POTATOES

Note: Although the recipes contained in this book have been tested by the manufacturers and have been carefully edited by the publisher, the publisher and the manufacturers cannot be held responsible for any ill effects caused by errors in the recipes, or by spoiled ingredients, unsanitary conditions, incorrect preparation procedures or any other cause beyond their control.

GOLDEN PARMESAN POTATOES

**2 lbs (910 g) new potatoes,
cut into quarters**
⅓ cup (80 ml) olive oil
1½ tsp (8 ml) Italian seasoning
2 cloves garlic, minced
**1 cup (240 ml) KRAFT 100%
Grated Parmesan Cheese**

Heat oven to 400°F (205°C). Toss
potatoes with oil, seasoning and garlic.
Add cheese; mix lightly. Place in
15x10x1-inch baking pan. Bake 45
minutes. Serves 8.

*Approximate nutritional analysis per serving:
Calories 234, Protein 7 g,
Carbohydrates 23 g, Fat 13 g,
Cholesterol 10 mg, Sodium 238 mg*

***Opposite: Golden
Parmesan Potatoes***

CALIFORNIA CHEESE POTATOES

**1 cup (240 ml) CALIFORNIA
ripe olive wedges**
**½ cup (120 ml) minced
red bell pepper**
**1 tsp (5 ml) minced
jalapeño pepper**
**3 cups (720 ml) sliced cooked
red skin potatoes**
1 tsp (5 ml) garlic salt
½ tsp (1 ml) white pepper
**¼ cup (60 ml) butter or
margarine**
3 tbs (45 ml) flour
1¾ cups (415 ml) milk
**1 cup (240 ml) grated
cheddar cheese**

Combine first 6 ingredients. Stir gently
to mix well. Melt butter over medium
heat. Add flour. Stir just until mixture
is golden, about 5 minutes. Add milk
gradually, stirring with wire whip.
Heat to boil. Reduce heat to simmer.
Simmer, stirring occasionally, for 20
minutes. Add cheese. Stir just until
melted. Add sauce to reserved olive
mixture. Transfer to shallow casserole
dish sprayed with nonstick spray. Bake
uncovered in preheated 350°F (180°C)
oven until golden brown and bubbly,
about 25-30 minutes. Serves 6.

*Approximate nutritional analysis per serving:
Calories 140, Protein 2 g,
Carbohydrates 14 g, Fat 9 g,
Cholesterol 21 mg, Sodium 305 mg*

POTATO AND APPLE SAUTÉ

**2 medium baking potatoes,
peeled and diced**
4 strips bacon, diced
3 tbs (45 ml) olive oil
**½ cup (120 ml) BLUE DIAMOND
Chopped Natural Almonds**
1 cup (240 ml) chopped onion
**1 small, tart green apple, peeled,
cored, and diced**
1 tsp (5 ml) sugar
½ tsp (3 ml) salt
1 tsp (5 ml) black pepper

Cook potatoes in salted, boiling water
until barely tender. Drain and reserve.
Sauté bacon in oil until it begins to
soften and turns translucent. Add
almonds and sauté until almonds are
crisp. Remove bacon and almonds with
a slotted spoon. Drain on paper towel.
In fat remaining in pan, sauté onion
until translucent. Add potatoes and
sauté until potatoes and onions start to
turn golden. Add apples and continue
to cook until apples are cooked but still
hold their shape. Return bacon and
almonds to pan. Sprinkle with sugar
and salt. Sauté 1-2 minutes longer until
sugar dissolves. Stir in pepper. Serves 6.

*Approximate nutritional analysis per serving:
Calories 213, Protein 5 g,
Carbohydrates 18 g, Fat 15 g,
Cholesterol 4 mg, Sodium 249 mg*

VEGETABLE CHEESE BAKED POTATO

3 - 3 oz (540 g) large baking potatoes
2 tbs (30 ml) skim milk
¼ cup (60 ml) sliced green onion
¼ tsp (1 ml) pepper
½ cup (120 ml) broccoli flowerets
½ cup (120 ml) sweet red pepper, cut into strips
½ cup (120 ml) cauliflower flowerets
½ cup (120 ml) water
½ lb (230 g) HEALTHY CHOICE Fat Free Pasteurized Process Cheese Loaf, cut into 1-inch cubes
½ cup (120 ml) skim milk
¼ tsp (1 ml) dill weed

Heat oven to 350°F (180°C). Clean and scrub potatoes. Prick several times with fork. Bake directly on oven rack for 1 hour or until softened. Remove from oven and cut potatoes lengthwise in half. Holding each potato half in a towel, scoop out center leaving ¼-inch shell. With mixer, beat together cooked potato, 2 tbs skim milk, green onions, and pepper; beat until smooth. Fill potato shells with potato mixture and keep warm.

Cook broccoli, red pepper slices and cauliflower in water until crisp-tender. Drain. In same saucepan, place cheese cubes and milk. Cook over medium heat, stirring occasionally, until cheese melts. Stir in vegetables and dill weed. Serve over potatoes. Serves 6.

Approximate nutritional analysis per serving: Calories 103, Protein 10 g, Carbohydrates 16 g, Fat 0 g, Cholesterol 7 mg, Sodium 547 mg

SALINAS VALLEY POTATO TOPPER

1 tbs (15 ml) margarine or butter
½ cup (120 ml) chopped fresh broccoli flowerets
1 cup (240 ml) DANNON Plain Nonfat or Lowfat Yogurt
¼ cup (60 ml) shredded part-skim mozzarella cheese
paprika

In a small heavy saucepan over medium heat melt margarine. Add broccoli; cook and stir just until tender. Remove from heat. Stir in yogurt and mozzarella. To serve, spoon onto baked potato halves and sprinkle with paprika. Serves 10.

Approximate nutritional analysis per 1 tbs serving: Calories 10, Protein 2 g, Carbohydrates 2 g, Fat 2 g, Cholesterol 6 mg, Sodium 31 mg

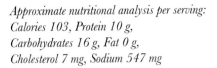

Vegetable Cheese Baked Potato

ZUCCHINI POTATO LATKES

2 zucchini
**4 large potatoes, peeled,
quartered or cut to fit
processor feed tube.
(Place in bowl of water
to avoid browning.)***
**1 large onion, peeled and
quartered**
3 large eggs
3 tbs (45 ml) flour
1 tbs (15 ml) chopped dill
salt and pepper to taste
vegetable oil to fry

*Note: If using food processor, use steel
blade on half and grater on rest to get
best consistency.

In food processor, fitted with the grater,
grate the zucchini. Squeeze out extra
liquid and place in a large bowl. Grate
half the potatoes and squeeze out
liquid. Add potatoes to the zucchini,
add eggs and flour. In the processor
fitted with the metal blade, grate onion
and remaining potato. Add this to the
zucchini potato mixture. Add dill, salt
and pepper to taste. Stir to blend well.

In a large heavy skillet heat $\frac{1}{8}$-$\frac{1}{4}$-
inch vegetable oil. With a tablespoon,
spoon mixture into hot oil, brown on
both sides. Drain on brown paper or
paper towels. Serve hot with
applesauce. Serves 8.

*Approximate nutritional analysis per serving
w/o applesauce: Calories 145, Protein 5 g,
Carbohydrates 20 g, Fat 6 g,
Cholesterol 80 mg, Sodium 29 mg*

Courtesy of the Empire Kosher Poultry
Test Kitchens.

Zucchini Potato Latkes

POTATOES WITH OLIVE AIOLI

2 lbs (910 g) small potatoes
2 tbs (30 ml) lemon juice
1 tbs (15 ml) Dijon mustard
1 egg yolk
1 tsp (5 ml) minced garlic
⅔ cup (160 ml) olive oil
1 tsp (5 ml) chopped fresh
    rosemary leaves
½ cup (120 ml) whole pitted
    CALIFORNIA ripe olives
chopped fresh parsley or herbs

Cover potatoes with water in large saucepan, cover, bring to boil and simmer for 15-20 minutes, or until barely tender. Meanwhile, combine lemon juice, mustard, egg yolk and garlic in electric blender and whir until smooth. Continue whirring, slowly adding oil. Turn off blender, add rosemary and olives then "pulse," off and on, until olives are finely chopped but not pureed. Slice hot cooked potatoes, turn onto serving platter and ribbon sauce down center. Sprinkle with parsley. Serves 6.

Approximate nutritional analysis per serving:
Calories 363, Protein 3 g,
Carbohydrates 32 g, Fat 26 g,
Cholesterol 35 mg, Sodium 103 mg

Potatoes with Olive Aioli

SAVORY MASHED POTATOES

1 tbs (15 ml) olive oil
1 tbs (15 ml) minced garlic
4 cups (960 ml) water
4 medium russet potatoes,
    peeled and cut into quarters
1 cup (240 ml) DANNON Plain
    Nonfat or Lowfat Yogurt
¼ cup (60 ml) milk
¼ cup (60 ml) sliced scallions or
    green onions
1 tsp (5 ml) salt
¼ tsp (1 ml) freshly ground
    pepper

In a large heavy saucepan or Dutch oven heat oil over medium-low heat. Add garlic; cook and stir 1 minute, stirring constantly, until fragrant but not browned. Add water and potatoes. Cover and bring to a boil over high heat. Reduce heat to medium-low and simmer 15-20 minutes or until potatoes are very tender. Drain well. Return potatoes to saucepan and mash. Add yogurt and milk and stir until creamy. Stir in scallions, salt and pepper. Serve immediately. Serves 8.

Approximate nutritional analysis per serving:
Calories 138, Protein 4 g,
Carbohydrates 26 g, Fat 3 g,
Cholesterol 3 mg, Sodium 296 mg

HERBED CHEESE MASHED POTATOES

2 tbs (30 ml) FLEISCHMANN'S Margarine
¼ cup (60 ml) chopped scallions
2 cloves garlic, minced
2 lbs (910 g) potatoes, peeled, cubed and cooked
½ cup (120 ml) nonfat yogurt
½ cup (120 ml) skim milk
2 oz (60 g) reduced fat Jarlsberg cheese, grated

In large saucepan, melt margarine. Add scallions and garlic; cook until tender. Add hot cooked potatoes, yogurt, milk and cheese. Mash until smooth and well blended. Serve immediately. Serves 6.

Approximate nutritional analysis per serving: Calories 214, Protein 6 g, Carbohydrates 33 g, Fat 5 g, Cholesterol 5 mg, Sodium 105 mg

Herbed Cheese Mashed Potatoes

TEXAS POTATO TOPPER

1 cup (240 ml) DANNON Plain Nonfat or Lowfat Yogurt
⅓ cup (80 ml) mild or medium chunky salsa
⅓ cup (80 ml) chopped stuffed green olives

In a small bowl combine yogurt, salsa and olives. Cover; chill until ready to serve. To serve, spoon onto baked potato halves. Serves 10.

Approximate nutritional analysis per 1 tbs serving: Calories 10, Protein 1 g, Carbohydrates 2g, Fat < 1 g, Cholesterol 1 mg, Sodium 91 mg

DAKOTA POTATO TOPPER

**1 cup (240 ml) DANNON Plain
    Nonfat or Lowfat Yogurt
3 tbs (45 ml) bacon bits
2 tsp (10 ml) prepared white
    horseradish**

In a small bowl combine yogurt, bacon bits and horseradish. Cover; chill until ready to serve. To serve, spoon onto baked potato halves. Serves 8.

Approximate nutritional analysis per 1 tbs serving: Calories 10, Protein 2 g, Carbohydrates 2 g, Fat 0 g, Cholesterol 3 mg, Sodium 46 mg

Dakota Potato Topper

BAKED POTATO LUNCH

Top a baked potato with **LIGHT & LEAN 97** ham or turkey cuts, a little low fat cheese, your favorite vegetables and a dollop of light sour cream for a healthy, satisfying meal. Add chives or parsley for some extra color and zest.

OVEN-ROASTED POTATOES

**1 lb (455 g) small new potatoes
1 red bell pepper, coarsely
    chopped
2 tbs (30 ml) soy oil
2 tbs (30 ml) chopped fresh
    rosemary
4 cloves garlic, minced
¼ cup (60 ml) sliced shallots
salt and pepper to taste**

Preheat oven to 475°F (246°C). Cut potatoes into wedges. In a bowl, combine the rest of the ingredients. Toss well with the potatoes. Arrange the potatoes in a single layer on cookie sheet and bake for 30-35 minutes until tender and lightly browned, tossing 2-3 times during baking. Serves 4.

Approximate nutritional analysis per serving: Calories 161, Protein 4 g, Carbohydrates 28 g, Fat 4 g, Cholesterol 0 mg, Sodium 8 mg

Courtesy of the National Potato Board

Opposite: Oven-Roasted Potatoes

LITTLE ITALY POTATO TOPPER

1 cup (240 ml) DANNON Plain
    Nonfat or Lowfat Yogurt
½ cup (120 ml) tomato, chopped
2 tbs (30 ml) grated Parmesan
    cheese
1 tbs (15 ml) chopped fresh basil
    leaves *or*
    ½ tsp (3 ml) dried basil
1 tbs (15 ml) fresh oregano *or*
    ¼ tsp (1 ml) dried oregano
¼ tsp (1 ml) salt

In small bowl combine yogurt, tomato, cheese, basil, oregano and salt. Cover; chill until ready to serve. To serve, spoon onto baked potato halves. Serves 10.

Approximate nutritional analysis per 1 tbs serving: Calories 10, Protein 2 g, Carbohydrates 2 g, Fat < 1 g, Cholesterol 2 mg, Sodium 93 mg

Little Italy Potato Topper

MASHED SWEET NEW YEAR POTATOES

1 lb (455 g) sweet potatoes,
    peeled and cubed
2 lbs (910 g) all-purpose potatoes,
    peeled and cubed
1 tbs (15 ml) margarine
¾-1 cup (180-240 ml) kosher
    chicken broth
salt and pepper, to taste
1 tbs (15 ml) chopped fresh
    Italian parsley

Place the potatoes in a large saucepan, cover with cold water and bring to a boil. Reduce heat, maintain a slight boil and cook 20-30 minutes or until tender. Drain potatoes, return them to saucepan and shake pan over low heat to remove remaining moisture. Transfer potatoes to a large bowl or an electric mixer and begin mashing by hand or slowly with mixer. Add broth, margarine, salt and pepper to the mixture. Beat until just smooth, lumps are OK. Stir in parsley and serve at once or keep warm in a pan over hot water. Serves 8.

Approximate nutritional analysis per serving: Calories 170, Protein 3 g, Carbohydrates 37 g, Fat 2 g, Cholesterol 0 mg, Sodium 32 mg

Courtesy of the Empire Kosher Poultry Test Kitchens.

MICROWAVING LOUISIANA YAMS

Microwaved yams have a different texture and flavor from yams cooked conventionally. They do not develop the sweet, syrupy taste of yams baked conventionally. Some people like them and others prefer baking yams conventionally, freezing them and reheating in the microwave. Yams may be microwaved for use in recipes calling for cooked yams.

To microwave yams, scrub them and prick with a fork or knife. This allows steam to escape and prevents the potato from popping. Arrangement is most important. To cook evenly, yams are placed in a circular arrangement with the smaller ends toward the center. Place in microwave on paper towel. Rearrange once during cooking time. Let stand three minutes to complete cooking. Dry or old potatoes do not microwave well whole. Peel and dice them before microwaving.

MICROWAVE TIME ON HIGH

1 potato	4-6 minutes
2 potatoes	6-8 minutes
3 potatoes	8-12 minutes
4 potatoes	12-16 minutes

Approximate nutritional analysis per yam: Calories 158, Protein 2 g, Carbohydrates 37 g, Fat 0 g, Cholesterol 0 mg, Sodium 20 mg

Courtesy of the Louisiana Sweet Potato Commission.

MASHED GREEN CHILI POTATOES

12 medium red new potatoes, peeled
2 tsp (10 ml) beef bouillon granules
4 large garlic cloves
1 - 4¼ oz can (135 g) CHI-CHI'S Diced Green Chilies, drained
2 tbs (30 ml) butter or margarine, if desired

In Dutch oven or large saucepan, place potatoes, bouillon and whole garlic cloves. Cover with water; bring to a boil. Reduce heat to low. Simmer 30-35 minutes or until potatoes are very tender. Remove potatoes and garlic to a large bowl. Mash with potato masher until there are few lumps, adding some of the cooking water as necessary to keep mixture moist. Stir in chilies. Stir in butter, if desired. Serves 5.

Approximate nutritional analysis per serving: Calories 90, Protein 3 g, Carbohydrates 20 g, Fat 0 g, Cholesterol 0 mg, Sodium 140 mg

Mashed Green Chili Potatoes

YAMS WITH ORANGES

6 yams or sweet potatoes, fully cooked and cooled

2 navel oranges, thinly sliced

¼-¾ cup (120-180 ml) butter

¾ cup (180 ml) brown sugar

1 cup (240 ml) FLORIDA'S NATURAL Brand Orange Juice

1 cup (240 ml) chopped fresh or frozen cranberries

2 tbs (30 ml) fresh lemon juice, or more to taste

Preheat oven to 375°F (190°C).

Peel the sweet potatoes and slice thinly. Place one layer in a shallow buttered baking dish. Top with a layer of orange slices. Dot generously with butter and sprinkle with sugar. Continue, making 3 layers, ending with a layer of potatoes, butter and sugar.

Mix the FLORIDA'S NATURAL Brand Orange Juice and cranberries with the lemon juice and pour over the potatoes. Bake until a pleasant syrup has formed and the top is tinged with brown, 1½ hours. Serves 8.

Approximate nutritional analysis per serving: Calories 341, Protein 3 g, Carbohydrates 58 g, Fat 12 g, Cholesterol 31 mg, Sodium 23 mg

Above: Yams with Oranges

SWEET POTATO TOPPER

1 cup (240 ml) LAND O LAKES
    No-Fat, Light or Regular
    Sour Cream
2 tsp (10 ml) dried basil leaves
1 cup (240 ml) water
2 cups (480 ml) chopped broccoli
2 medium carrots, thinly sliced
2 tsp (10 ml) LAND O LAKES
    Butter, softened
½ tsp (3 ml) Italian herb
    seasoning
½ tsp (3 ml) garlic powder
1 small onion, coarsely chopped
1 small red pepper, cut into
    ½-inch pieces
4 hot roasted sweet potatoes,
    cut in half lengthwise
2 oz (60 g) light cheddar or
    mozzarella cheese, shredded

In small bowl stir together No-Fat Sour Cream and basil; set aside. In 10-inch nonstick skillet bring water to a full boil; add broccoli and carrots. Cook until crispy tender, 2-3 minutes; drain. In same skillet melt butter until sizzling; stir in Italian herb seasoning and garlic powder. Add broccoli, carrots, onion and red pepper. Cook over medium heat, stirring constantly until vegetables are crisply tender, 2-3 minutes. Set aside; keep warm. Heat broiler. Place roasted potatoes on broiler pan. Spread No-Fat Sour Cream mixture evenly over potato halves. Divide vegetable mixture evenly among potato halves; top each with 1 tbs shredded cheese. Broil 3-5 inches from heat until cheese is melted, 1-3 minutes. Serves 8.

Approximate nutritional analysis per serving:
Calories 130, Protein 6 g,
Carbohydrates 23 g, Fat 2 g,
Cholesterol 10 mg, Sodium 120 mg

TWICE-BAKED SWEET POTATOES

2 sweet potatoes
2 tsp (10 ml) reduced fat butter
    or margarine
⅓ cup (80 ml) skim milk
¼ tsp (1 ml) cinnamon
¼ tsp (1 ml) nutmeg
dash ginger

Wrap sweet potatoes in aluminum foil, pierce, and bake in an iron skillet, Dutch oven, or pan. Bake 20 minutes at 500°F (260°C), lower oven to 400°F (205°C), bake until tender. Let sweet potato cool. Cut in half, remove pulp, save skins. Mix pulp with ⅓ cup skim milk, cinnamon, nutmeg, and ginger. Add 2 tsp of reduced fat butter or margarine to pulp mixture. Beat pulp mixture with an electric mixer until smooth. Spoon pulp into shells, bake on baking sheet for 10-15 minutes at 350°F (180°C). Serves 4.

Approximate nutritional analysis per serving:
Calories 133, Protein 2 g,
Carbohydrates 29 g, Fat 1 g,
Cholesterol 3 mg, Sodium 24 mg

CANDIED SWEET POTATOES

2 large sweet potatoes
3 tbs (45 ml) brown sugar
1 tbs (15 ml) reduced fat butter
    or margarine
¼ cup (60 ml) orange juice
¼ tsp (1 ml) cinnamon
¼ tsp (1 m l) nutmeg

Wash sweet potatoes, peel and slice into ½-inch slices. Place sweet potatoes in baking pan. Arrange slices in a single layer, ½-inch apart. Mix brown sugar, orange juice, spices together. Pour mixture on top of sweet potato slices. Dot sweet potatoes with reduced fat butter or margarine. Cover and bake at 375°F (190°C) for 30 minutes, or until tender. Serves 4.

Approximate nutritional analysis per serving:
Calories 141, Protein 1 g,
Carbohydrates 30 g, Fat 2 g,
Cholesterol 5 mg, Sodium 13 mg

Courtesy of the Louisiana Sweet Potato Commission.

PRUNE-STUFFED YAMS

6 medium LOUISIANA yams
1 tbs (15 ml) grated orange peel
½ cup (120 ml) orange juice
¼ tsp (1 ml) salt
¼ cup (60 ml) butter or
  margarine
1 cup (240 ml) cooked prunes,
  pitted and halved
2 tbs (30 ml) slivered almonds

Bake yams in 400°F (205°C) oven
15 minutes. Lower temperature to
375°F (190°C) and bake 45 minutes or
until tender. Score lengthwise and
crosswise and scoop out yam centers,
leaving ¼-inch shells. Mash yams; add
orange peel and juice, salt and butter;
whip well. Fold in prunes. Divide
equally among yam shells; sprinkle with
almonds. Return to oven to heat
through, about 5-10 minutes. Serves 6.

Approximate nutritional analysis per serving:
Calories 289, Protein 4 g,
Carbohydrates 49 g, Fat 10 g,
Cholesterol 21 mg, Sodium 111 mg

LOUISIANA YAM PATTYCAKES

4 medium LOUISIANA yams,
  cooked, peeled and mashed
  ***or* 2 - 16 oz cans (960 g)**
  LOUISIANA yams, drained
  and mashed
1 cup (240 ml) toasted rice cereal,
  Rice Krispies
⅓ cup (80 ml) finely chopped
  celery
¼ cup (60 ml) finely chopped
  onion
2 tbs (30 ml) flour, plus extra for
  baking sheet
¾ tsp (4 ml) salt
dash pepper
1 egg
3 tbs (45 ml) butter or margarine
3 tbs (45 ml) salad oil
apple butter or apple sauce

Combine yams, cereal, celery, onion,
2 tbs flour, salt, pepper and the egg;
mix well. Drop by rounded tablespoon-
fuls onto lightly floured baking sheet;
shape into patties. Chill for about
1 hour to firm.

In large skillet, heat butter and oil
together. With spatula, lift each patty
off baking sheet and lightly coat with
flour. Fry in butter and oil over
medium-low heat until lightly browned
on each side, about 2-3 minutes per
side, turning once. Serve with apple
butter or apple sauce. Serves 20.

Approximate nutritional analysis per patty:
Calories 78, Protein 1 g, Carbohydrates 9 g,
Fat 4 g, Cholesterol 15 mg, Sodium 106 mg

Prune-Stuffed Yams

SWEET POTATO PONE

2 cups (480 ml) grated raw yams
½ cup (120 ml) sugar
¼ cup (60 ml) Karo or
    Cane syrup
½ tsp (3 ml) cinnamon
1 egg
¼ cup (60 ml) flour
½ tsp (3 ml) baking powder
½ stick butter
¼ cup (60 ml) evaporated milk
½ tsp (3 ml) vanilla extract

Mix all ingredients. Pour into casserole
and bake at 350°F (180°C) for 45
minutes to 1 hour. Serves 10.

Approximate nutritional analysis per serving:
Calories 194, Protein 2 g,
Carbohydrates 34 g, Fat 6 g,
Cholesterol 36 mg, Sodium 44 mg

Courtesy of Louisiana Sweet Potatoes.

**Green Peas, Potatoes
and Prosciutto**

Sweet Potato Pone

GREEN PEAS, POTATOES AND PROSCIUTTO

2 cups (480 ml) diced peeled
    potatoes
1 cup (240 ml) fresh or frozen
    tiny green peas
1 tbs (15 ml) minced prosciutto
    or ham
2 tsp (10 ml) BERTOLLI Classico
    or Extra Virgin Olive Oil
freshly ground black pepper

Cook the potatoes in boiling salted
water until almost tender, about 8
minutes. Add the peas and cook
1 minute. Drain. Add the prosciutto
and olive oil to the vegetable mixture.
Season with black pepper and serve.
Serves 4.

Approximate nutritional analysis per serving:
Calories 115, Protein 4 g,
Carbohydrates 19 g, Fat 3 g,
Cholesterol 1 mg, Sodium 34 mg

HEIDELBERG POTATO SALAD

4 slices bacon
1 tbs (15 ml) flour
1 tbs (15 ml) sugar
½ tsp (3 ml) salt
½ tsp (3 ml) **MCCORMICK'S**
    dry mustard
¼-½ tsp (1-3 ml) celery seed
½ cup (120 ml) water
¼ cup (60 ml) vinegar
6 hard-cooked eggs, sliced
3 medium potatoes, cooked,
    peeled and chopped
¼ cup (60 ml) chopped green
    onions with tops
celery leaves, optional

In 10-inch skillet over medium heat, cook bacon until crisp. Remove from pan, drain, crumble and set aside. Pour off all but 1 tbs bacon drippings. Blend in flour, sugar, salt, mustard and celery seed. Cook, stirring constantly, until mixture is smooth and bubbly. Combine water and vinegar. Stir into flour mixture all at once. Cook until mixture boils and is smooth and thickened.

Reserve 2 center egg slices for garnish. Chop remaining eggs. Add chopped eggs, potatoes, onions and reserved bacon to sauce. Gently stir to mix. Heat to serving temperature. Garnish with reserved egg slices and celery leaves, if desired. Serves 4.

Approximate nutritional analysis per serving:
Calories 258, Protein 13 g,
Carbohydrates 27 g, Fat 11 g,
Cholesterol 323 mg, Sodium 468 mg

Above: Heidelberg Potato Salad

CHUNKY NEW POTATO SALAD WITH TOMATOES

2 medium FLORIDA tomatoes
2 lbs (910 g) small new potatoes, cut in 1½-inch pieces
1 cup (240 ml) unpeeled cucumber, thinly sliced
¾ cup (180 ml) chopped green bell pepper
¾ cup (180 ml) thinly sliced celery
⅓ cup (80 ml) sliced scallions (green onions)
⅓ cup (80 ml) mayonnaise
⅓ cup (80 ml) dairy sour cream
1¼ tsp (6 ml) tarragon leaves, crushed
¾ tsp (4 ml) salt
½ tsp (3 ml) ground black pepper

In a medium saucepan bring potatoes and enough water to cover to a boil; reduce heat and simmer, covered, until potatoes are tender, 10-12 minutes; drain. In a large bowl place potatoes, cucumber, green pepper, celery and scallions. Make dressing by combining mayonnaise, sour cream, tarragon, salt and black pepper. Cut each tomato into 8 wedges; cut wedges in halves (makes about 2 cups). Just before serving gently stir in tomatoes. Line a salad bowl with tomatoes or lettuce as garnish. Serves 6.

Approximate nutritional analysis per serving:
Calories 258, Protein 4 g,
Carbohydrates 33 g, Fat 13 g,
Cholesterol 13 mg, Sodium 382 mg

CHOICE POTATO SALAD

3 medium potatoes
1 small onion, minced
1 tbs (15 ml) fresh parsley, minced
2 tbs (30 ml) celery, minced
1 tbs (15 ml) green pepper, minced
1 hard-cooked egg, chopped
1 clove garlic, minced
1 tsp (5 ml) Creole or regular mustard
¼ cup (60 ml) mayonnaise, regular or light
1 tbs (15 ml) cider or wine vinegar
1 tbs (15 ml) salad oil
1 tsp (5 ml) celery seed or caraway seed
1 tsp (5 ml) salt
1 tsp (5 ml) IMPERIAL Granulated Sugar
¼ tsp (1 ml) pepper

Boil potatoes in jackets until done in centers; peel, dice, place in mixing bowl. Add remaining ingredients and mix well. Serve while warm or chill first. If desired, decorate with extra sliced hard-cooked egg and parsley sprigs. Serves 4.

Approximate nutritional analysis per serving:
Calories 245, Protein 4 g,
Carbohydrates 23 g, Fat 16 g,
Cholesterol 61 mg, Sodium 635 mg

LENTIL, RED PEPPER AND POTATO SALAD

2 cups (480 ml) cooked lentils
1 cup (240 ml) cooked potatoes, diced ¼ inch
½ cup (120 ml) cooked fresh or thawed frozen green peas
½ cup (120 ml) red bell pepper, finely chopped
¼ cup (60 ml) red onion, chopped
¼ cup (60 ml) celery, chopped
1 tbs (15 ml) Italian, flat leaf, parsley, finely chopped
1 tbs (15 ml) basil, finely chopped
2 tbs (30 ml) red wine vinegar
2 tbs (30 ml) BERTOLLI Extra Virgin Olive Oil
salt and freshly ground black pepper

Combine the lentils, potatoes, peas, red peppers, red onion, celery, parsley and basil in a large bowl. Whisk the vinegar, oil, salt and pepper in a separate bowl; add to the lentil mixture; toss and serve. Serves 6.

Approximate nutritional analysis per serving:
Calories 157, Protein 7 g,
Carbohydrates 22 g, Fat 5 g,
Cholesterol 0 mg, Sodium 9 mg

GALLEY YAMS AND APPLES

1 cup (240 ml) diagonally-sliced
    celery
¼ cup (60 ml) butter or
    margarine
4 LOUISIANA yams, cooked,
    peeled and halved *or*
    2 - 16 oz cans (960 g)
    LOUISIANA yams, drained
2½ cups (590 ml) canned
    apple slices
1 tbs (15 ml) chopped chives
½ tsp (3 ml) grated lemon peel

In same skillet, sauté celery in butter 5 minutes. Add remaining ingredients and cook covered 5 minutes or until heated through. Serves 8.

Approximate nutritional analysis per serving: Calories 175, Protein 2 g, Carbohydrates 30 g, Fat 6 g, Cholesterol 16 mg, Sodium 26 mg

Opposite: Galley Yams and Apples

HEARTY POTATO SOUP

1 cup (240 ml) green onions,
    white part, thinly sliced
2 tbs (30 ml) butter, margarine
    or oil
1 large potato, peeled and diced
2 cups (480 ml) chicken stock
    or 2 chicken bouillon cubes
    and 2 cups (480 ml) water
dash white pepper
dash nutmeg
salt to taste
⅛ tsp (.5 ml) IMPERIAL
    Granulated Sugar
1 - 5 oz can (150 ml) evaporated
    milk

Sauté green onions in butter, margarine or oil. Add diced potato, chicken stock, white pepper, nutmeg, salt, IMPERIAL Granulated Sugar. Bring to a boil, turn down heat and simmer until potatoes are soft; about 10 minutes. Blend in blender until smooth. Add evaporated milk and heat. Can be served cold. Yields 1 qt.

Approximate nutritional analysis per 1 cup serving: Calories 157, Protein 6 g, Carbohydrates 13 g, Fat 9 g, Cholesterol 10 mg, Sodium 507 mg

CREAMY POTATO SOUP

3 medium potatoes, cubed
2 - 13¾ oz cans (825 ml)
    COLLEGE INN
    Lower Salt Chicken Broth
½ cup (120 ml) onion, chopped
½ cup (120 ml) green pepper,
    chopped
1 tbs (15 ml) FLEISCHMANN'S
    Margarine
¼ cup (60 ml) all purpose flour
2 cups (480 ml) skim milk
parsley, for garnish
48 HARVEST CRISPS 5-Grain
    Crackers

In large saucepan, over medium-high heat, heat potatoes and chicken broth to a boil; reduce heat. Cover; simmer 15 minutes or until potatoes are tender. Meanwhile, in medium skillet, over medium heat, sauté onion and green pepper in margarine until tender but not browned; stir in flour. Gradually whisk in milk; cook and stir until thickened. Stir into potato mixture; cool slightly. Remove 1 cup potatoes and ½ cup liquid to food processor or blender container; blend until smooth. Stir potato puree into soup; cook and stir until heated through. Garnish each serving with parsley if desired. Serve hot with crackers. Serves 8.

Approximate nutritional analysis per serving soup plus 6 crackers: Calories 166, Fat 1 g, Cholesterol 4 mg, Sodium 457 mg

PEAR AND POTATO SALAD

1 cup (240 ml) BLUE DIAMOND Blanched Slivered Almonds
1 tbs (15 ml) olive oil
½ cup (120 ml) mayonnaise
2 cloves garlic, chopped finely
**¼ tsp (1 ml) grated, fresh ginger
    or ⅛ tsp (.5 ml) powdered
    ginger**
½ tsp (3 ml) salt
¼ tsp (1 ml) pepper
**½ cup (120 ml) chopped,
    fresh parsley**
**½ lb (230 g) new potatoes,
    peeled and diced**
**1 lb (455 g) slightly firm pears,
    peeled, cored,
    diced and tossed with:**
1 tbs (15 ml) lemon juice
1 medium red bell pepper, diced
**½ cup (120 ml) thinly sliced
    green onion,
    including part of green**

Sauté almonds in oil until golden; reserve. Combine mayonnaise, garlic, ginger, salt and pepper. Fold in parsley; reserve. Cook potatoes in salted, boiling water until just tender. Take care not to overcook. Drain, and while still warm, combine with dressing. Cool to room temperature. Fold in pears, red bell pepper and green onion. Chill. Just before serving, fold in almonds. Serves 6.

Approximate nutritional analysis per serving:
Calories 264, Protein 6 g,
Carbohydrates 27 g, Fat 17 g,
Cholesterol 10 mg, Sodium 209 mg

Above right: Purrusalda

Pear and Potato Salad

PURRUSALDA
Leek and Potato Soup

**½ lb (230 g) leeks, chopped,
    including some green tops**
¼ cup (60 ml) GOYA Olive Oil
**½ lb (230 g) potatoes, peeled
    and cubed**
2 cloves garlic, chopped
4 cups (960 ml) water
**2 packets GOYA Chicken
    bouillon**
pepper to taste

In a large saucepan or soup pot, sauté leeks in olive oil over low heat, stirring continuously, until leeks are soft. Add potato cubes and garlic and sauté lightly, 1-2 minutes. Add water and bouillon. Bring to a boil, reduce heat, and simmer gently for approximately 20 minutes or until potatoes are tender. Add pepper to taste. Serves 4.

Approximate nutritional analysis per serving:
Calories 213, Protein 2 g,
Carbohydrates 20 g, Fat 14 g,
Cholesterol < 1 mg, Sodium 572 mg

CHICKEN CHOWDER WITH POTATO DUMPLINGS

2 cups (480 ml) cooked chicken,
   cut up
1 cup (240 ml) frozen or canned
   whole kernel corn
2 cups (480 ml) skim milk
½ tsp (3 ml) salt
1 - 16 oz can (480 g) cream-style
   corn
1 - 2 oz jar (60 g) sliced
   pimientos, drained
1 cup (240 ml) BISQUICK
   Reduced Fat Baking Mix
⅓ cup (80 ml) BETTY CROCKER
   Potato Buds
   Mashed Potatoes, dry
2 tbs (30 ml) skim milk
1 tbs (15 ml) fresh parsley,
   chopped
   or 1 tsp (5 ml) dried parsley
   flakes
2 egg whites
   or ¼ cup (60 ml) cholesterol
free egg product

Mix chicken, whole kernel corn, 2 cups milk, the salt, creamed corn and pimientos in 4-qt Dutch oven. Heat to boiling over medium heat, stirring occasionally. Beat baking mix, potatoes, 2 tbs milk, the parsley and egg whites until dough forms (dough will be very stiff). Turn dough onto surface well dusted with baking mix; roll in baking mix to coat. Knead about 30 times or until no longer sticky. Pat dough into ½-inch squares. Drop squares into gently boiling chowder. Cook uncovered 6-8 minutes or until dumplings are slightly puffy and dry inside. Sprinkle with parsley if desired. Serves 6.

Approximate nutritional analysis per serving: Calories 290, Protein 22 g, Carbohydrates 39 g, Fat 5 g, Cholesterol 45 mg, Sodium 730 mg

Chicken Chowder with Potato Dumplings

COCKTAILS AT TIFFANY'S

1 cup (240 ml) cooked wild rice
1 cup (240 ml) raw potato,
   shredded
⅓ cup (80 ml) CALIFORNIA
   golden raisins
1 egg, beaten
2 tbs (30 ml) chives, snipped
2 tbs (30 ml) half and half
1 tbs (15 ml) butter or margarine,
   melted
3 tbs (45 ml) flour
¼ tsp (1 ml) salt
¼ tsp (1 ml) pepper
sour cream
golden and black caviars,
   optional

In bowl combine rice, potato, raisins, egg, chives, half and half, and butter. Stir in flour, salt and pepper; mix to blend. Spoon into hot, oiled skillet, a few at at time, to make 2-3-inch pancakes. Fry until golden on both sides. Serve hot with sour cream and caviars. Serves 4.

Approximate nutritional analysis per serving, without sour cream and caviar: Calories 153, Protein 5 g, Carbohydrates 23 g, Fat 5 g, Cholesterol 64 mg, Sodium 185 mg

Approximate nutritional analysis per serving, with 1 tbs sour cream and 1 tsp caviar: Calories 198, Protein 6 g, Carbohydrates 24 g, Fat 9 g, Cholesterol 101 mg, Sodium 272 mg

HAZELNUT POTATO BISCUITS

½ lb (120 g) butter
2 cups (480 ml) flour
3 tsp (15 ml) baking powder
¼ tsp (1 ml) garlic powder
½ tsp (3 ml) salt
1 tsp (5 ml) pepper, coarsely
    ground
1 cup (240 ml) mashed potatoes
¾ cup (180 ml) OREGON
    hazelnuts, chopped
1 egg yolk mixed with
    1 tsp (5 ml) water

Blend butter, flour, baking powder, garlic, salt and pepper to form crumbly mixture. Add potatoes and mix quickly. Mix in hazelnuts. After a few minutes, roll dough onto a floured board, fold once and chill for 20 minutes. Knead, roll and chill 3 more times. Heat oven to 375°F (190°C). Roll out dough to 1 inch thick. Cut into 1½-inch rounds. Criss-cross top of biscuits with knife blade, then brush with egg yolk and water mixture. Place on greased baking sheet and bake for 20-25 minutes. Biscuits are done when they are shiny gold. Serve with red wine, cocktails or a hearty soup. Serves 12.

Approximate nutritional analysis per serving: Calories 272, Protein 4 g, Carbohydrates 20 g, Fat 21 g, Cholesterol 59 mg, Sodium 329 mg

Hazelnut Potato Biscuits

ROOTS AND TUBERS SOUP

8 cups (1.9 L) chicken broth
    or bouillon
1 - 14½ oz can (435 g) stewed
    tomatoes
1 - 6 oz can (180 g) tomato paste
1 medium onion, chopped
1 carrot, sliced
1 small turnip, peeled and cubed
1 small rutabaga, peeled and
    cubed
1 parsnip, peeled and cubed
2 stalks celery, sliced
2 medium potatoes, cubed
1½ cups (355 ml) green cabbage,
    chopped
2 bay leaves
1½ tsp (8 ml) MCCORMICK'S
    ground sage
½ tsp (3 ml) black pepper

In 6-qt pot combine all ingredients; bring to a boil. Cover, reduce heat and simmer about 25-30 minutes or until vegetables are tender. Serve hot. Soup can be stored, covered, in refrigerator up to 1 week. Serves 10.

Approximate nutritional analysis per serving: Calories 141, Protein 6 g, Carbohydrates 25 g, Fat 3 g, Cholesterol 8 mg, Sodium 872 mg

Opposite: Roots and Tubers Soup

POTACOS

9 baking potatoes
**CHEF PAUL PRUDHOMME'S
     Meat Magic**
1 - 12 oz container (360 g)
     cottage cheese
1 tbs (15 ml) apple cider vinegar

SEASONING MIX:
1½ tsp (8 ml) ground cumin
¾ tsp (4 ml) dried leaf oregano
1½ tsp (8 ml) dried leaf cilantro
¾ tsp (4 ml) ground cinnamon
¼ tsp (1 ml) nutmeg
1 tsp (5 ml) salt

FILLING:
1½ cups (355 ml) onions,
     chopped
1 cup (240 ml) celery, chopped
1½ cups (355 ml) green bell
     peppers, chopped
2 tbs (30 ml) CHEF PAUL
     PRUDHOMME'S
     Poultry Magic
1 tbs (15 ml) fresh garlic, minced
3 cups (720 ml) chicken stock,
     defatted, in all
1 lb (455 g) lean ground turkey
1 tbs (15 ml) ground roasted
     Ultimo chili peppers
1 tbs (15 ml) ground roasted
     CALIFORNIA
     beauty chili peppers
4 tbs (60 ml) yellow cornmeal
½ cup (120 ml) canned green
     chilies
chopped shredded lettuce
1 cup plus 2 tbs (270 ml)
     tomatoes, finely chopped
9 tbs (135 ml) onions, chopped
6 tbs (90 ml) low-moisture
     part-skim mozzarella cheese

If you can't find roasted chili peppers, substitute 2 tbs (30 ml) commercial chili powder.

Preheat oven to 375°F (190°C). Rinse and cut potatoes in half lengthwise, then cut a small slice off the bottom of each half. Place the potatoes on a baking sheet in oven for 1 hour, or until brown, and the potato comes easily out of the skin. Let cool at least ½ hour. Using a sharp knife, cut the insides of the potato away from the skin (save for another use), leaving as thin a shell as you can without leaving holes. (This may take a little practice.) Sprinkle potato shells with a little Meat Magic and put back in the oven for about 15-20 minutes, or until skins are brown and crisp.

Combine seasoning mix ingredients thoroughly in a small bowl.

To make mock sour cream, place cottage cheese in blender and process until smooth. Add vinegar and process again until completely blended.

To make the filling, preheat a large heavy skillet over high heat. Add 1½ cups chopped onions, the chopped celery and green bell peppers, and cook 2 minutes. Add Poultry Magic and the seasoning mix and cook 4 minutes, stirring once to distribute the seasoning evenly. Add the minced garlic and ½ cup stock. Scrape the bottom and cook 9 minutes, stirring occasionally. Push the cooked vegetables to the edges of the skillet, making a clearing in the center. Add the chopped turkey to the center of the skillet and cook 9 minutes, breaking the meat up with a wooden spoon, turning occasionally to brown it evenly and eventually incorporating it into the vegetable mixture. Add the chili powders and the cornmeal and cook 2 minutes, scraping the bottom of the pan, because the cornmeal will stick and form a brown crust. Add ½ cup stock, scrape the bottom well and spread the turkey mixture over the bottom of the skillet. Stir occasionally and cook 3 minutes, or until the mixture is sticking hard. Add 1 cup stock, scrape the bottom well and cook 3 minutes. Stir in the chopped chilies and cook 2 minutes. Add ½ cup stock, stir well and cook 5 minutes. Add the remaining ½ cup stock and cook 8 minutes, stirring and scraping the bottom well as the mixture sticks. Remove from heat.

Place crisp potato shells on a baking sheet. Line the bottom of each with a little shredded lettuce. Add 1 tsp chopped tomatoes and ½ tbs finely chopped onions. Fill with 2 tbs meat mixture and top with ⅓ tbs shredded mozzarella. Place baking sheet under preheated broiler about 1 minute or until cheese is brown and bubbly. Garnish with 1½ tbs mock sour cream. Serves 18.

*Approximate nutritional analysis per serving:
Calories 226, Protein 14 g,
Carbohydrates 32 g, Fat 5 g,
Cholesterol 21 mg, Sodium 439 mg*